THE VIKINGS

by Robert Nicholson and Claire Watts

Editorial Consultant: Gareth Binns, Education Officer,
York Archaeological Trust & Council for
British Archaeology

FRANKLIN WATTS
in association with
TWO-CAN

First published in this edition in 1991 by
Franklin Watts
96 Leonard Street
London EC2A 4RH

Copyright © Two-Can Publishing Ltd, 1991
Text copyright © Robert Nicholson, 1991
Design by Millions Design

Printed and bound in Hong Kong

A CIP catalogue record for this book is available from the British Library

ISBN: 0-7496-0467-0

THE VIKINGS

Photographic credits:
Werner Forman: p. 3, p. 6, p. 7, p. 8, p. 9, p. 10, p. 11, p. 12, p. 13, p. 16, p. 17, p. 20 (top)
p. 21, p. 23, p. 30 (top), p. 32 (bottom); Toby Maudsley: p. 20 (craft) p. 22; Ronald Sheridan:
p. 30 (middle); York Archaeological Trust: p. 19, p. 24

Illustration credits:
Kevin Maddison: p. 9, p. 11, pp. 12-13, p. 14, p. 17, pp. 18-19, pp. 22-23, p. 24
Maxine Hamil cover: pp. 25-29

Contents

All words marked in **bold** can be found in the glossary.

▼ Eric the Red founded a
settlement in Greenland.

▲ The Vikings were the first
Europeans to reach America.

Lindisfarne was an island
whose wealthy, unprotected
monastery was an easy target for
the Vikings.

"on 8 june the ravages of heathen
men miserably destroyed god's
church on lindisfarne with plunder
and slaughter..."

(ANGLO-SAXON CHRONICLE, 793)

The Viking World

The first glimpse many European people had
of the Vikings was when the fierce dragon-
heads of the Viking longships appeared off
their coasts. No-one was prepared for the
invading warriors and few countries could
resist the Vikings. From the first attacks in
793, Viking raids were a frequent occurrence
all over north-western Europe for the next
200 years.

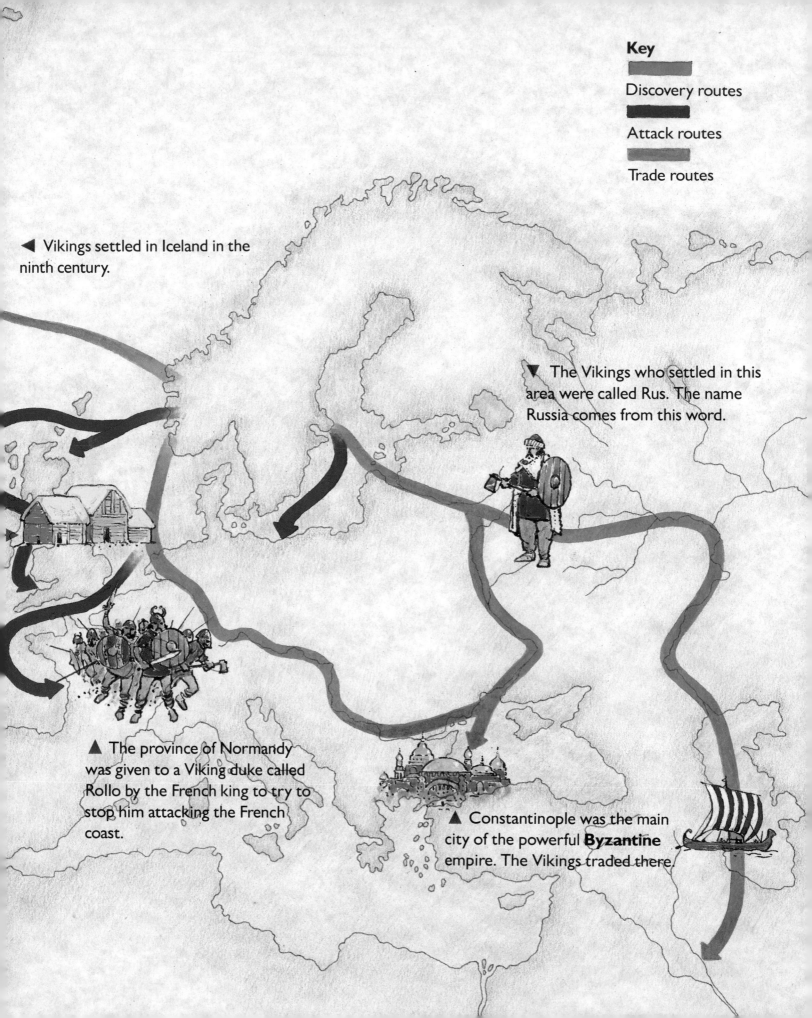

Key

Discovery routes

Attack routes

Trade routes

◄ Vikings settled in Iceland in the ninth century.

▼ The Vikings who settled in this area were called Rus. The name Russia comes from this word.

▲ The province of Normandy was given to a Viking duke called Rollo by the French king to try to stop him attacking the French coast.

▲ Constantinople was the main city of the powerful **Byzantine** empire. The Vikings traded there.

Viking Lands

The Vikings came from the countries which are now called Sweden, Norway and Denmark. These lands are cold and bleak, with deep rivers, rocky coasts and mountains. There was not enough good farm land to produce sufficient food for all the Vikings, even though they also fished and hunted wild animals.

Many Vikings chose to leave their homes rather than try to farm the meagre land. They set out to seek riches using their skills as seamen and warriors.

Viking lands were divided into several different kingdoms. The richest and most powerful men became leaders and were called kings and dukes. These leaders would sometimes call all the **free men** to a meeting known as the **Allthing** where they would discuss plans about expeditions to other countries or make decisions about local problems. There were often wars between the different kingdoms, particularly over pieces of good land.

▼ Men gathering for the Allthing.

▼ The narrow, deep-watered fjords of **Scandinavia** form perfect natural harbours.

Pirates or Traders?

Pirates

The Vikings attacked lands around them, particularly Britain and France, stealing food and treasures and carrying people off to become slaves. People who lived in isolated areas on the coast or on islands were terrified of the Vikings' attacks. They were mostly farmers, and were not used to defending themselves and their families. They added to their daily prayers the words "God deliver us from the fury of the **Northmen.**"

▲ Viking helmets like this one have been found at a number of gravesites in Europe. Soldiers were often buried with all their weapons because the Vikings believed they would need them on the way to heaven.

▼ Rope was wrapped around the hilt of Viking swords to protect the warrior's hand.

Traders

In certain places the Vikings got food and goods by trading rather than by attacking and stealing property. They usually chose to trade rather than attack when the inhabitants were stronger or more organised and could defend themselves better. Viking traders travelled as far south as the Black Sea trading their furs, jewellery and slaves for spices and wine.

▶ Goods were sold by weight of gold or silver rather than for a number of coins. Merchants used tiny portable scales to weigh the gold or silver. If they needed to give change they would break up the coins.

Longships

The Vikings were superb seamen and used ships for travelling on the lakes, seas and fjords of Scandinavia as well as further afield. The ships were measured by the number of oars they had, the smallest, a **faering**, with 4 and the largest, a **longship**, with about 32. A big longship might be nearly 30 m long and would travel at up to 32 km per hour under full sail. Ships were so important to the Vikings that their language contained dozens of ways of saying "ship".

The Vikings managed to navigate without any of the modern equipment that is used today. They found their way by watching the stars and Sun as well as familiar landmarks like islands and mountains. They also looked out for birds which are found in different places at different times of year, like puffins and fulmars.

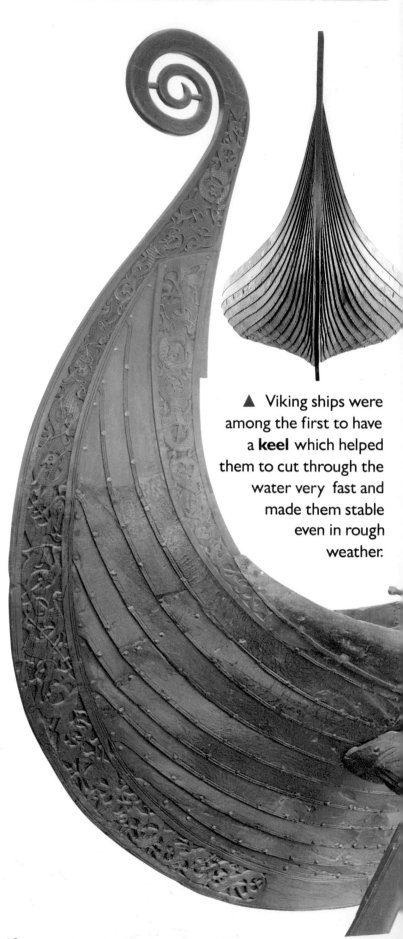

▲ Viking ships were among the first to have a **keel** which helped them to cut through the water very fast and made them stable even in rough weather.

▲ Oars were used if the sail was not up, when there was no wind or on inland waters. Each rower sat on a box which held his belongings and a waterproof reindeer-skin sleeping bag.

► The gaps between the oak planks of the ship were made waterproof by filling them with sheep's wool dipped in tar.

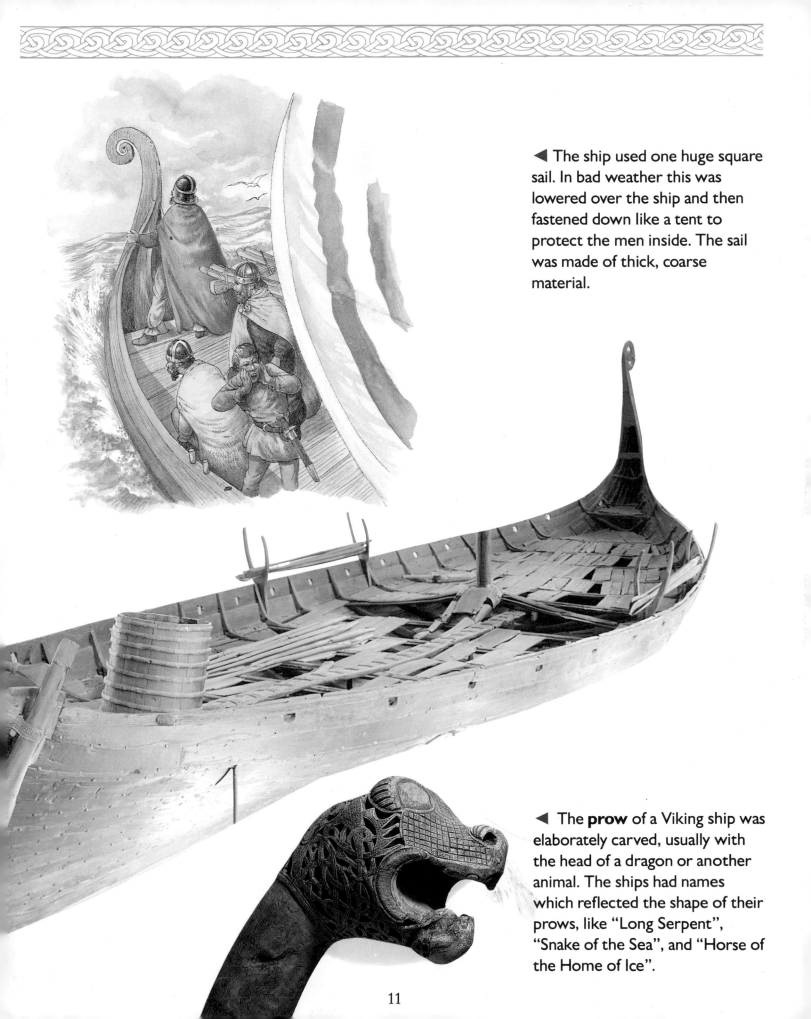

◀ The ship used one huge square sail. In bad weather this was lowered over the ship and then fastened down like a tent to protect the men inside. The sail was made of thick, coarse material.

◀ The **prow** of a Viking ship was elaborately carved, usually with the head of a dragon or another animal. The ships had names which reflected the shape of their prows, like "Long Serpent", "Snake of the Sea", and "Horse of the Home of Ice".

Heroes

The Vikings admired bold and fearless men and their heroes were all soldiers, sailors or explorers. The deeds of heroes were told again and again until they became more like myths than real historical fact.

Leif Ericson

Eric the Red's son Leif, who was known as "Lucky", arrived in northern America 500 years before Columbus reached the continent. He landed to the south of Newfoundland in a place which he called Markland. He travelled on south to a place called Vinland, which may have been south of modern New York. The Vikings left America after about two years when they were attacked by Indians.

King Cnut

In 1016 England had suffered 200 years of Viking raids, which had made the country very weak. When King Cnut of Denmark attacked England, the English king had just died and so Cnut took over. The English accepted him because he was a wise ruler and brought peace.

Harald Haardraade

As the fame of the Vikings spread throughout Europe, many kings paid Vikings to work in their armies. The Byzantine Emperor had an elite fighting force of Vikings called the **Varangarian Guard.** Harald Haardraade, or Hard-nose, was a famous member of the Guard, who later became king of Norway. He was the last Viking to land with an army in England.

Sagas and Runes

Viking children did not go to school to learn. Lessons came in the form of long stories, or **sagas**, which told the adventures of the gods or of great Viking heroes. These stories were important ways of teaching history, geography and navigation. Children would also learn whilst helping their parents around the house and farm.

Storytellers travelled around reciting sagas at feasts and festivals. They were especially sought after on dark, cold winter nights, when everyone sat inside around the fire.

▲ Some buildings were decorated with pictures from famous sagas. The wood carving above shows Sigurd the Dragon-Slayer attacking a dragon.

▲ This stone carving shows one of the tales of Odin. You can see Odin in the centre at the top, handing a sword to an old man.

The Futhark

The Viking alphabet, the **Futhark**, was quite different from ours. The letters, or **runes**, are made up mostly of straight lines. This is because they were usually carved into wood or stone and it is easier to carve straight lines than curves.

► These are all the runes of the Futhark. Underneath you can see how all the letters were pronounced. Try writing your name in runes – it's like a secret code!

The Viking Gods

The Vikings believed that there were lots of different gods who lived in a place called **Asgard.** Each one was responsible for a different thing, like war, travel or the home. In stories the gods were not perfect. They had very human qualities, and also human weaknesses like jealousy and greed.

If a Viking died fighting it was believed that he went to a hall in Asgard called **Vallhalla**, where everybody fought all day and feasted all night.

Thor

Some Important Gods

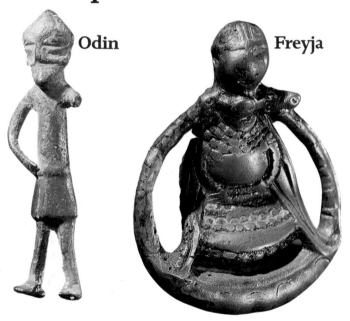

Odin   Freyja

THOR, the god of thunder, was the most popular god. He was short-tempered and a little stupid, but very good-hearted. He had the qualities that the Vikings thought most important: strength and determination.

ODIN or Woden was the god of war, who rode an eight-legged horse. He often doubted himself and spent too long trying to decide whether to do things or not.

FREY made sure that the sun shone, rain fell and the crops grew. He owned a magic boat which could carry all the gods at once, but folded up in his pocket when not needed.

FREYJA was Frey's sister. She was the goddess of love and war. She could turn herself into a bird by putting on a magic falcon-skin.

LOKI was half god, half fire-spirit. He caused the other gods a lot of trouble.

▲ When Viking warriors died their bodies were often placed in longships, which were buried or set alight and pushed out to sea.

► Towards the end of the Viking age the Vikings began to convert to Christianity. This is a mould made in the tenth century for making Christian crosses, but it could also be used for making copies of **Mjollnir**, Thor's hammer.

At Home

The Vikings were not only skilled soldiers, seamen and traders. Most Vikings were farmers and lived with their families, growing and making all the things they needed for their daily lives. Children helped their parents as soon as they were able to. Even very small children had their own jobs around the farm, like feeding the animals or gathering firewood.

Viking women worked on the farm and wove material for clothes and blankets on small looms. When their husbands were away fighting, they took care of the whole farm.

Viking houses were made of timber planks and woven branches, with turf or thatched roofs. Stone was used in places where there was no wood, like Shetland and Iceland. Inside, the houses were not divided into rooms. Areas were separated off by stretching cloth or skins between the pillars which supported the roof.

A typical farm would contain the family house, or more than one house if the family were large. There were also sheds for the animals, a workshop with a furnace for making metal tools, and small huts for slaves.

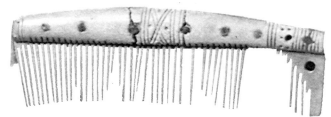

Rubbish!

● Viking homes were not as clean as our houses are. Meat bones and vegetable peelings might be left on the floor all winter and only cleared out in the spring.

● Rubbish was buried outside.

● All the Vikings had combs because they had lice in their hair.

Games

Viking children did not spend all their time helping their parents. They had some time to themselves for playing games and carving wooden toys. Girls and boys went skating in winter, using skates made of carved bone. These were strapped to the children's shoes with strips of leather.

When it was too dark and cold to go outside, Viking children may have played a game called **hnefatal**. This was a board game rather like chess but with simple pieces, like draughts.

Crafts

Vikings were very skilled craftsmen, making marvellous objects from stone, wood and metal. Many of the most beautiful objects were not made by specialist artists, but by ordinary people. A farmer might make a brooch using the same furnace he used to make his plough.

As there were no banks, people wore their wealth in the form of jewellery. This was the best way to keep it safe.

Smiths were very highly respected and often became very wealthy. Thor, one of the most important Viking gods, used a smith's hammer as his main weapon.

▲ Some jewellery was made specially for burial with a dead person. This arm-ring was found at a burial site.

Make Some Viking Jewellery

Look at the decoration on the Viking objects in this book. Can you see how all the figures are woven around one another? The Vikings loved to use complicated patterns for decoration.

Try making a bracelet or brooch using Viking designs. Modelling clay that you can bake hard in the oven is good for making jewellery.

◀ Use four balls of clay to make the heads.

▼ Roll out three long strands and plait them together.

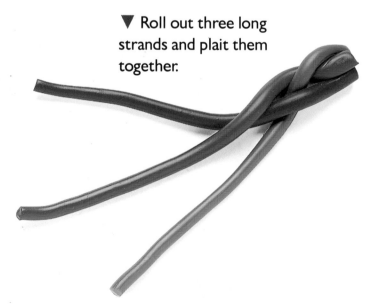

▼ This is a mould which was used to make part of a helmet. Once the mould was made, many helmets could be made with this pattern.

► This gold pendant was worn around the neck as a magical amulet. Look at the elaborate patterns that cover it.

► The symbol of Thor's hammer was used in much Viking jewellery. This hammer head is made in silver but many were much simpler than this.

Food

Finding food was a very important part of a Viking's life. Little of the land was fertile and the winters were very long and harsh, so as well as growing and raising food on their farms, the Vikings hunted and fished for food. They ate rich stews of beef or mutton from their farms, or fish and whale meat. They grew vegetables like cabbage, peas and beans and also ate wild leeks and garlic.

Trestle tables would be set up in the middle of the room for meals, and members of the family would sit on the same wooden benches that they slept on at night. They ate off rectangular wooden platters or from soapstone bowls, using spoons and the knives that were carried on their belts at all times.

The Vikings used drinking horns as well as cups. Because the horns did not have flat bottoms, they had to be passed on around the table until they were empty. A man who could drain a drinking horn at one go was very highly thought of! The usual drink was mead, a sweet beer made from honey.

Food Facts

● When the Vikings had no other grain they would use peas to make bread.
● Salt was made by boiling sea-water.
● The Vikings ate two meals a day: the **day meal** after the early farmwork and the **night meal** at the end of the day.

Cooking was done over an open hearth fire. Meat was roasted on huge spits, and stews were made in big iron cauldrons. Sometimes a **gridiron** made of coiled iron was used. Does it remind you of part of a modern cooker? Bread was baked in stone ovens or in the ashes of the fire.

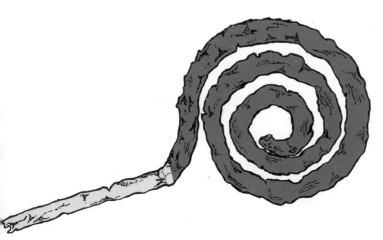

Bowls were made from pottery or soapstone.

Clothes

Most Viking clothes were made from coarse woollen cloth, although some rich people wore imported silk or linen. In winter people wore furs to keep warm.

Men wore an undershirt and breeches, covered by long woollen trousers and a tunic which reached to the knees. All this was held up with a leather belt. A purse and knife were carried on the belt.

Women wore long wool or linen dresses with a woollen tunic rather like an apron attached with brooches. Hanging from their belts they carried a knife and keys.

▲ Shoes were made from leather or goatskin, laced up with strips of leather.

Thor Visits the Land of the Giants

This story is part of a Viking saga. It is about Thor, the god of thunder, and the journey he set out on to prove his strength. The journey and the trials of strength would have been very familiar to the Vikings.

One summer day, Thor, Loki and their two servants set off to visit Utgard, the land of the giants. After a long journey, they arrived at the gates of Utgard to find them locked. Thor thumped and hammered on the gates, calling out for someone to come and and let them in, but Loki grinned and slipped through the bars, dragging the others after him. They walked into the great hall of Utgard. In the middle of the hall was a long table around which hundreds of giants were seated on benches, eating and drinking and making the most enormous noise. The giants all began to laugh as Thor marched up to the Giant King who was seated on a chair at the far end of the hall.

"Greetings, Giant King," said Thor, politely.

The Giant King sat chewing bones and did not even look at Thor. From time to time he tossed a bone over his shoulder and picked up a new one.

Thor spoke again, a little louder: "Greetings, Gi . . ."

The Giant King interrupted: "So you're the great thunder god Thor, are you? Well, you look like a scrawny little piece of work to me. I suppose you've come to test your strength?"

Thor was furious at the Giant King's rudeness, but it did not seem a very good idea to lose his temper when he was surrounded by giants.

"What skill would you like to challenge us with?" continued the Giant King.

Thor looked around him at the giants.

"I doubt if anyone here can drink as much as I can," Thor replied.

The Giant King signalled to a servant, who brought forward a huge drinking horn.

"This is the horn used by all my followers," he said. "A good drinker can finish it in one draught, and all here can down it in two at the most. Let us see what the great Thor can do!"

Thor took the horn. It was certainly not the largest he had ever drunk from. He raised it to his mouth and began to swallow. He felt sure he could drink it all, but he ran out of breath before the horn was empty. He looked into the horn and found that it was no less full than before. He drank a second time, and again had to stop for breath. This time the horn was no longer brimming full. He took a third draught, gulping down the liquid until he was sure he must empty the horn, but although the level was lower than before, the horn was by no means empty.

"You don't seem to be much of a drinker," said the Giant King. "Why not try your strength? Some of the younger giants like to test themselves by lifting my cat. We don't think this much of a feat, but perhaps you'd like to try?"

Standing beside the Giant King's chair was the most enormous cat Thor had ever seen. He braced himself and then put both arms under the cat and heaved. The cat simply arched its back. Thor heaved again and managed to make the cat lift one paw off the ground before he had to admit defeat.

"As I thought," said the Giant King scornfully. "You may be strong in Asgard and in the realms of men, but your strength is nothing here."

At this Thor grew angry. "I can match any of your men in a fight. Just let anyone here wrestle with me."

There was a roar of laughter from all the giants in the hall.

"Everyone here feels that wrestling with you would be too easy," said the Giant King. "Perhaps you could fight Elli, my foster mother."

A wrinkled old woman hobbled forward leaning on a stick. Thor thought that the Giant King was making fun of him until Elli threw down her stick and took hold of him. He knew at once that his strength would be sorely tested. They struggled and fought, but eventually Elli threw Thor off balance so that he landed on one knee.

"Enough, enough!" shouted the Giant King. "You have shown us that you have no strength as a wrestler either. As you pose no threat to us, you may eat with us and spend the night here in Utgard."

Thor and his companions were very hungry and tired after their long journey. When they had eaten, the tables were pushed back, and they spread their bedding in a space on the floor among the giants.

Thor awoke early, before any of the giants, and roused his companions.

"Come, let's go before the giants wake up," he whispered.

They tiptoed over the sleeping giants and out of the gates of Utgard. To their surprise, they found the Giant King already outside waiting for them. He walked with them across the plain for a while.

At last he stopped: "This is where I must leave you. Thor, do not feel too badly about your failures last night."

Thor was puzzled. "But I have never before been so soundly beaten," he said.

The Giant King replied: "You were not competing in a fair fight. I feared your strength, so I used magic to deceive you. The other end of the horn that you drank from was in the sea. When you reach the shore you will see just how much you have lowered its level. The cat you lifted was really the giant serpent whose body is wrapped around the world. You managed to lift it until its back touched the sky. And as for Elli, it was a wonder you withstood her for so long. You see, Elli is Old Age, which defeats all men in time."

Thor was furious that he had been tricked. He seized his hammer Mjollnir and swung it around his head, but the Giant King and Utgard had vanished, as if they had never been.

29

How We Know

Have you ever wondered how, although the Vikings lived over 1000 years ago, we know so much about their daily lives?

Evidence from the Ground

Certain objects have been found preserved in wet earth or water. Often these are very ordinary objects which were thrown away by the Vikings because they were broken or not needed. Archaeologists piece them together and work out how the Vikings used them.

Some important Vikings were buried in ships full of their possessions. When these ships are discovered, archaeologists can gain a lot of information about the Vikings.

Evidence from Books

Many of the stories told by the Vikings were written down, and so it is quite easy to find out who the important gods were and what various historical figures did. We even know that when Eric the Red discovered Greenland, he gave it that name in spite of its cold iciness because "many would want to go there if it had so promising a name".

Evidence around us

Many place names in Europe were originally Viking names, and so we can tell where the Vikings settled.

The whole of Normandy in France was taken over by the Vikings, and the name means land of the Northmen.

In Britain many place names have the Viking endings "-thorpe" and "-by", like Scunthorpe and Grimsby. Can you find any others on a map?

And what about our days of the week? Did you know that Wednesday was originally Woden's day, and Thursday Thor's day?

Glossary

Allthing
a council of free men which met when problems arose. This was the only form of government the Vikings had.

Asgard
the place where the Vikings believed that their gods lived, and where they would go when they died.

Byzantine
the strongest world power at the time of the Vikings was the Byzantine empire in the east which lasted from the 6th to the 15th century.

day meal
the first meal of the day, eaten after the early farmwork had been done.

free men
all the men who were not slaves. Slaves were usually people who had been captured on raids.

faering
the smallest type of Viking ship, with four oars.

Futhark
the runic alphabet used by the Vikings. The word is taken from the sound of the first six letters.

gridiron
a coiled metal strip which was placed in the fire to heat pots on.

hnefatal
a board game played by the Vikings.

keel
the long timber which forms the lowest part of a ship and helps it to balance.

longship
the long, low ships used by Vikings.

Mjollnir
Thor's hammer. He carried it with him at all times.

night meal
the meal eaten after all the work was done, when it began to grow dark.

Northmen
most of the people the Vikings attacked or traded with knew them as "Northmen". "Viking" was a term they used to describe themselves.

prow
the front end of a ship.

rune
a letter of the Viking alphabet. Runes are made up of straight lines because they were intended to be carved on wood or stone.

saga
storytelling adventure of gods or heroes. Although sagas were usually passed on by word of mouth, some were written down.

Scandinavia
The group of countries which include Denmark, Norway, Sweden and Iceland.

Vallhalla
the hall in Asgard where warriors hoped to go when they died. Here they could fight all day and feast all night.

Varangarian Guard
a section of the Byzantine army made up of Vikings. The Varangarian Guard were the Emperor's bodyguard.

Index

For more information about TWO-CAN books, write to TWO-CAN Publishing, 346 Old Street, London EC1V 9NQ.

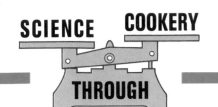

SCIENCE COOKERY

THROUGH

Liquids in Action

Peter Mellett
Jane Rossiter

FRANKLIN WATTS

London • New York • Sydney • Toronto

Franklin Watts
96 Leonard Street
London EC2A 4RH

Franklin Watts
14 Mars Road
Lane Cove
NSW 2066

UK ISBN: 0 7496 0926 5

10 9 8 7 6 5 4 3 2 1

Senior editor: Hazel Poole
Series editor: Jane Walker
Designer: Ann Samuel
Illustrator: Annabel Milne
Photographer: Michael Stannard
Consultant: Margaret Whalley

The publisher would like to
thank the following children
for their participation in the
photography of this book:
Tom Brownrigg, Caroline
Rossiter, Alexander Rossiter,
Katie Samuel and Corinne
Smith-Williams.

A CIP catalogue record for
this book is available from
the British Library

Typeset by Spectrum, London
Printed in Singapore

Contents

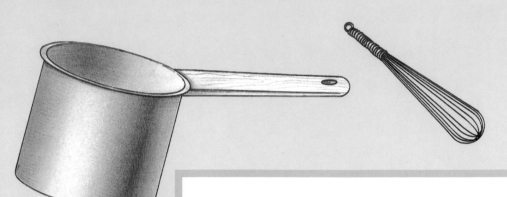

Introduction

Science Through Cookery is a new, simple and fun approach to learning about science. In each book you will not only read about science, but you will also have first-hand experience of real science. By linking science topics with simple cookery recipes, you can learn about science and at the same time cook some delicious recipes. Science is fun when you finish up eating the results of your work!

About this book

In **Liquids in Action** you can read about water and other liquids. The book finds out how liquids behave when heated or when a solid substance is added. Simple explanations of difficult terms, such as density and surface tension, help you to understand why some liquids will not mix.

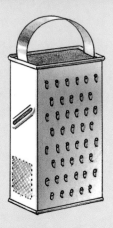

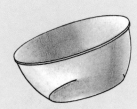

Liquids in Action explains important scientific principles with the help of clearly labelled diagrams and illustrations. The recipes offer a practical opportunity to gain a better understanding of the science you have just read about.

Each recipe has been carefully selected and written so that the cookery can be done with a minimum amount of adult supervision. Where the help of an adult is needed, for example when boiling a pan of water, this is clearly indicated.

The ingredients and equipment you will need are listed at the beginning of each recipe. They are easily obtainable and no specialist equipment is required. The step-by-step format of the recipes is easy to follow. Each step is illustrated with a photograph.

At the end of the book you will find a page of Further things to do. These are fun experiments and activities which are linked to many of the science concepts discussed in the book. A glossary of terms and an index are provided at the end of the book.

What is a liquid?

Eggs, bread, air, spoons and custard and everything else in the world are made up from matter. Matter can exist in three states: solid, liquid or gas.

Wooden or metal spoons are solids. They are firm and keep their shape. When food is cooking, it gives off gases that we can smell. Gases spread out and completely fill the space they are in.

Milk, lemonade, water and gravy are all liquids. They are runny and we can pour them from one container to

Banana milk shake

Ingredients
400ml milk
1 banana
2 teaspoons sugar
a little grated nutmeg

Equipment

a measuring jug
a liquidizer or food processor
a chopping board
a knife
a teaspoon
2 glasses

1 Measure the milk in the measuring jug. Peel the banana and chop it into pieces.

2 Put the milk, banana and sugar into the liquidizer or food processor. Switch it on and whizz the ingredients together until the mixture is thick and frothy.

another. Liquids spread out to fill the lowest part of their containers. Liquids also have flat and level surfaces.

Matter takes up space and has mass. You can measure the mass of anything by weighing it. Some substances can exist in all three states. Depending on the temperature, water can exist as solid ice, as liquid water or as a gas called steam.

Milk is a liquid, but 95 per cent of milk is actually water. A tomato is a solid, but 95 per cent of it is water. Your body is about 65 per cent water. During your lifetime, you will take in about 60,000 litres of water.

All your food contains water. Look how much water is in these foods:
- bread 30%
- steak 70%
- lettuce 95%
- potato 80%
- orange 85%

3 Pour the milk shake into two glasses, and sprinkle it with some grated nutmeg.

From a liquid to a gas

A kettle of boiling water gives off hot, steamy clouds. But if you look carefully, you will see a clear space right next to the spout. This clear space appears to be empty, but it actually contains a colourless gas called steam. When the water inside the kettle is heated, some of it turns into steam. The change from a liquid to a gas is called evaporation.

As the steam moves away from the spout, it cools and changes into tiny droplets of water. The change from a gas to a liquid is called condensation. The water droplets make up the steamy clouds you can see.

cooled steam changes to water

steam

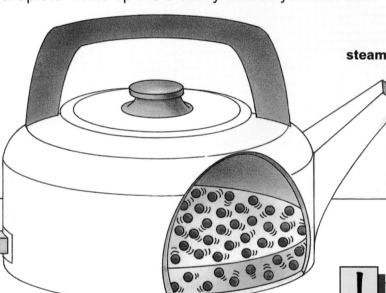

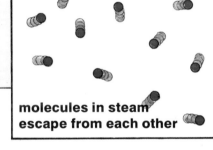

molecules in steam escape from each other

Every substance is made up from tiny invisible pieces, or particles, called atoms. In most liquids, the atoms are joined together in separate groups called molecules.

Water is made from molecules. The molecules are all the same, and they are moving about freely all the time. The hotter the water, the faster the molecules are moving. Some of the molecules in boiling water are moving so fast that they escape completely from each other. The result is steam.

Evaporated milk is made by heating milk in a special container. Some of the water in the milk evaporates. It turns into a gas which is pumped away. The rest of the milk contains fats and solids which do not evaporate. They stay in the container and become evaporated milk.

In hot countries, sea water is used to make sea salt. The sea water flows into shallow pools. Heat from the Sun evaporates the water, leaving behind solid salt.

Steamed vegetable parcels

Ingredients
4 large cabbage leaves
1 carrot
1 leek
1 stick of celery
salt and pepper

Equipment

a large saucepan, with a steamer
a chopping board
a knife
a bowl
a slotted spoon
4 cocktail sticks

1 Half fill the saucepan with water. Ask an adult to help you boil the water. Wash all the vegetables, and scrub the carrot and celery.

2 Cut the hard stalk out of the end of the cabbage leaves.

3 Chop the carrot, leek and celery into very small pieces. Put these into the bowl and season well with salt and pepper. Mix the ingredients together.

4 When the saucepan of water is boiling, ask an adult to help you lower the cabbage leaves into it. Boil for 1 minute. Carefully remove with the slotted spoon, and place on the chopping board.

5 Divide the vegetable mixture into four portions, and place some mixture on each leaf. Roll up the leaves to make parcels. Push a cocktail stick through each parcel.

6 Place the parcels carefully into the steamer and put it over the pan of simmering water. Cover the steamer with a lid.

7 Steam the parcels for 20 minutes. Remove them from the steamer and serve at once. The vegetables will be cooked but still quite firm.

From a liquid to a solid

Water is a runny liquid. But if you put some water in the freezer, it will turn into solid ice. What makes this happen?

The molecules in a liquid rush about and move freely past each other. When you cool a liquid, some energy is removed from it, making the molecules move more slowly.

When water is very cold, the molecules do not have enough energy to move about freely. They join together in groups and gently vibrate backwards and forwards. These groups make up crystals of ice. The crystals contain water molecules which are fixed in a regular pattern.

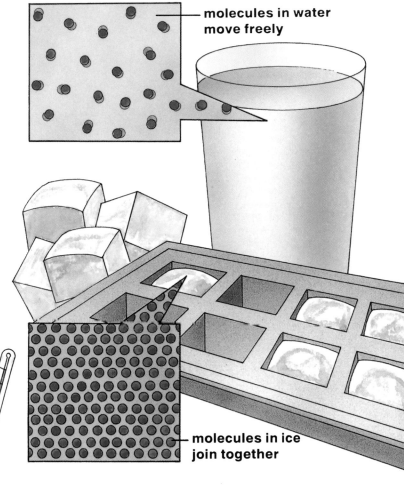

molecules in water move freely

molecules in ice join together

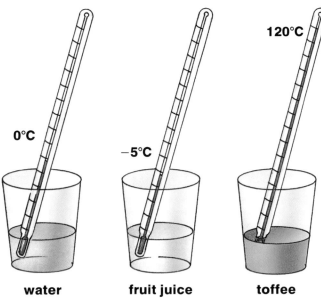

0°C — water

−5°C — fruit juice

120°C — toffee

Different liquids freeze at different temperatures. Water freezes at 0 degrees Celsius (0°C for short). Fruit juice freezes at an even lower temperature (−5°C). Hot liquid toffee freezes when the temperature falls below 120°C.

There were no electric refrigerators 200 years ago, but rich people still wanted cold drinks in the summer.

During the winter, their servants cut lumps of ice from a frozen river. They stored the ice in ice houses, which were large underground rooms covered with heavy blocks of stone and soil. Bales of straw were placed around the ice to keep out the warmth. The ice stayed solid for many months in the ice houses.

Apricot yoghurt ice

Ingredients
400g tinned apricots
300g natural yoghurt
2 egg whites
2 tablespoons soft brown sugar

Equipment

a tin opener
a sieve
2 small bowls
a chopping board
a knife
a large bowl
an electric or hand whisk
a tablespoon
a plastic container with a lid

1 Ask an adult to set the freezer, or the ice compartment of the fridge, to its coldest setting. Open the tin of apricots. Place the sieve over a bowl and pour the apricots into the sieve.

2 Chop the drained apricots into small pieces. Spoon the yoghurt into a bowl and add the chopped apricots. Mix until the ingredients are thoroughly combined.

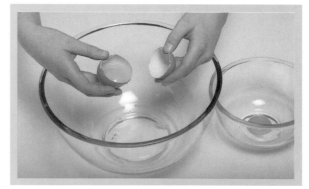

3 Separate the egg whites from the yolks. (You cannot whisk the whites properly if any yolk is left behind.) Put the egg whites into the large bowl.

4 Whisk the egg whites until they are stiff and no longer move about when you tilt the bowl.

5 Whisk the sugar into the egg whites, one tablespoon at a time.

6 Pour the apricot and yoghurt mixture into the bowl of beaten egg whites. Mix together gently but thoroughly until the ingredients are combined.

7 Spoon the mixture into the plastic container and freeze until it is solid (about 4 hours).

Jam is made by boiling a mixture of fruit and sugar. Some kinds of fruit contain too much water. If this water is not removed, the jam will be too runny.

When the mixture is boiled in a pan, the extra water turns into a gas called steam. Heat from the cooker gives energy to the molecules in the jam mixture. This makes them move about more quickly. Water molecules are smaller and lighter than the other molecules in the mixture. As the mixture boils, the water evaporates and some molecules escape as steam.

If you boil milk very gently for a long time, all the water eventually escapes. The result is a white solid. This solid is the part of milk that does not boil away as steam. When this solid is mixed with some liquid water, the result is milk.

Dried food keeps for a very long time. In hot countries, fish, coconut and fruits like dates can be dried in the sunshine. Peas can be dried in special ovens.

Dried milk and instant coffee powder are made by spray-drying. Liquid milk or liquid coffee sprays down through a tall tower. All the water evaporates from the liquid droplets as they fall, leaving behind the dried milk or coffee powder.

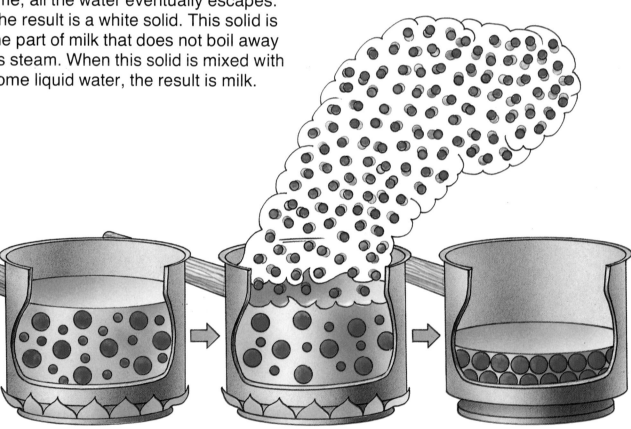

heat from flame gives energy to jam molecules

jam boils and water escapes as steam

level of jam goes down

Pasta with cheese sauce

Ingredients
150g pasta shapes
500ml water
3 tablespoons dried milk powder
50g margarine or butter
50g plain flour
100g cheese
salt and pepper

Equipment
a large saucepan
a small saucepan
a tablespoon
a measuring jug
a wire whisk
weighing scales
a cheese grater
a plate
a colander

1. Ask an adult to help you boil a large saucepan of water. Measure the dried milk powder into the measuring jug.

2. Fill the measuring jug with water to the 500-ml mark. Stir until the milk powder and water are thoroughly mixed. Grate the cheese onto a plate.

3. When the saucepan of water is boiling, carefully add the pasta shapes. Boil without a lid for 10–12 minutes. Ask an adult to help you drain the cooked pasta through a colander.

4. Weigh out the margarine or butter and the flour very accurately. Put them into the small saucepan and pour on the milk. Mix with the wire whisk. The mixture will look rather lumpy at this stage.

5 Over a medium to high heat, whisk the mixture all the time as the margarine or butter melts, and the sauce heats up.

6 When the sauce has started to boil and to thicken, turn the heat down low and simmer for 1 minute. Keep whisking all the time.

7 Take the pan off the cooker and add the cheese, salt and pepper. Mix well and let the cheese melt into the sauce. Add the cooked pasta, stir again and serve.

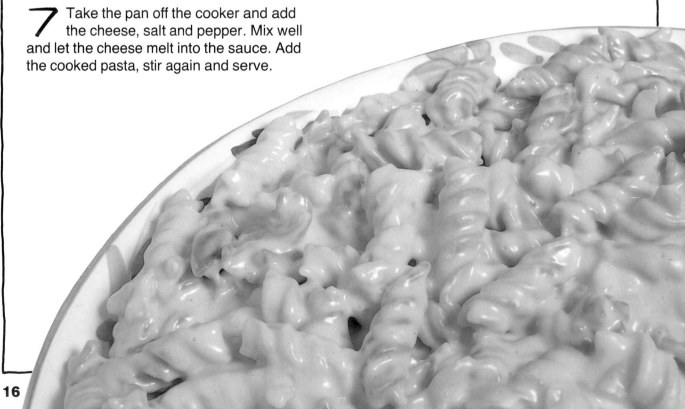

Measuring liquids

A recipe for bread will tell you to mix 700 grams of flour with 300 millilitres of water. The 700 grams measure the weight of the flour. The 300 millilitres measure the volume of the water. Volume tells you how much space is taken up by something.

You measure the volume of a liquid by pouring it into a clear glass or plastic container which has a scale marked on its side. The main unit of volume is the litre. The litre can be divided into smaller units. There are 100 centilitres (100 cl for short) and 1,000 millilitres (1,000 ml for short) in 1 litre.

- A millilitre is sometimes called a cubic centimetre, especially when it is used to talk about the volume of a solid.

- The volume of a lump of sugar is about 1 cubic centimetre (or 1 millilitre).

1,000 millilitres	= 1 litre
10 millilitres	= 1 centilitre
100 centilitres	= 1 litre
1 cubic centimetre	= 1 millilitre

Abbreviations

litre	= l
centilitre	= cl
millilitre	= ml
cubic centimetre	= cm^3

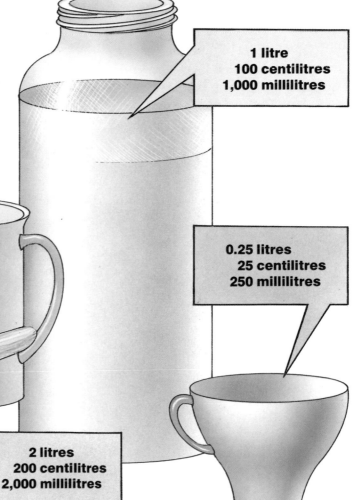

1 litre
100 centilitres
1,000 millilitres

0.3 litres
30 centilitres
300 millilitres

0.25 litres
25 centilitres
250 millilitres

2 litres
200 centilitres
2,000 millilitres

Making a solution

When you make a pot of tea, you pour boiling water onto the tea leaves and the water turns a clear golden-brown colour. This golden-brown liquid is a solution of tea. The colour changes because the water dissolves part of the tea leaves. This part is soluble. The leaves that are left at the bottom of the pot do not dissolve. That part is insoluble.

Salt is soluble in water. If you stir a spoonful of salt into a glass of water, the solid salt will slowly disappear as it dissolves. The result is a clear solution of salty water. But there is a limit to the amount of salt that a glass of water can dissolve. When the water cannot dissolve any more salt, it is saturated. Hot water can dissolve more salt more quickly than cold water.

Starch is insoluble in water. If you stir a spoonful of starch powder into a glass of water, the water will not dissolve the starch. The result will be a cloudy mixture called a suspension.

Many clear liquids that you can see through are solutions. Some solutions are made from solids dissolved in liquids. Liquid food colourings are solutions that contain powdered dyes dissolved in water.

Solutions can also be made from gases dissolved in liquids. Lemonade is a solution of carbon dioxide gas dissolved in sugary water. When you unscrew the top of a lemonade bottle, some of the dissolved gas escapes and the lemonade fizzes.

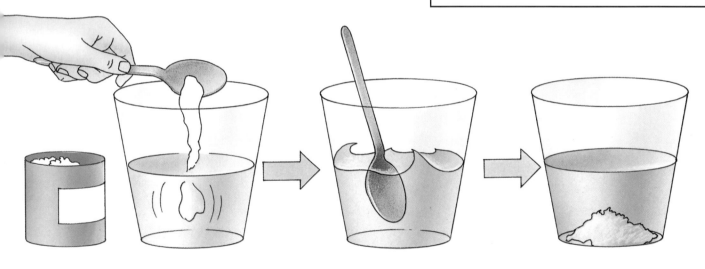

salt is added to water | **salt dissolves in water to make clear solution** | **no more salt will dissolve in saturated solution**

Butterscotch sauce

Ingredients
50g butter or margarine
4 tablespoons soft brown sugar
2 tablespoons golden syrup

Equipment

weighing scales
a small saucepan
a tablespoon
a wooden spoon

1 Weigh out the butter and put it into the saucepan. Measure the sugar and add it to the pan. Do the same with the golden syrup.

2 Heat the ingredients gently. Stir them with a wooden spoon until the sugar has dissolved and the butter has melted.

3 Make sure that the ingredients are mixed together well. Bring the mixture to the boil and let it bubble for 1 minute. Serve at once with ice cream or sponge pudding.

Filtering

You cook frozen peas by boiling them in water. The water is then removed by straining the peas in a sieve. The water runs away through holes that are too small to allow the peas to pass. The peas stay behind in the sieve, which works as a sort of filter.

A tea strainer is a filter. It has smaller holes than a sieve. As the tea pours through it, the strainer stops tea leaves from passing into your cup.

A coffee filter made from paper is full of tiny holes that are too small for you to see. The filter holds coffee beans which

Ghee (Indian butter)

Ingredients
250g butter

Equipment

a saucepan
a bowl
a piece of fine muslin
a sieve

1 Melt the butter in the saucepan over a medium heat. Do not let it bubble or burn.

2 Place the sieve over the bowl, and line it with the muslin.

have been ground into a gritty powder. When you pour boiling water onto the ground coffee, the water dissolves the taste and smell from the powder. The water then passes through the paper filter. Clear brown liquid coffee drips down into the coffee pot.

Some Japanese teapots are fitted with a filter in their spout. The filter is a bundle of thin twigs that trap the tea leaves as they enter the spout.

The water that comes out of our taps has been filtered at the water works. The filter is a huge tank that has a layer of stones and sand in the bottom. Water pours into the tank and passes down through this layer. The sand filters the water and traps any solid particles in it.

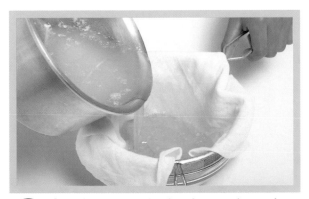

3 Carefully pour the hot butter through the sieve into the bowl. The white pieces in the butter will stay in the muslin. When the ghee cools, use it to fry spices, meat and other ingredients in Indian recipes.

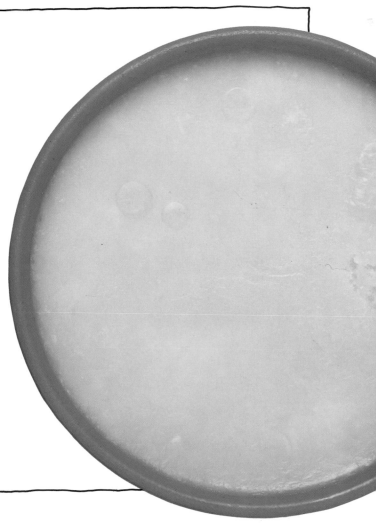

What is density?

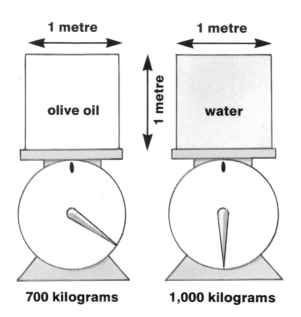

1 metre · olive oil · 1 metre · 700 kilograms

1 metre · water · 1 metre · 1,000 kilograms

Which is heavier – cooking oil or water? The answer depends on how much oil and water you measure. You must compare equal volumes of oil and water in order to answer the question.

Scientists compare different substances by measuring the mass of 1 cubic metre of each substance. They call this the density of the substance.

The density of water is 1,000 kilograms per cubic metre. This can be written as 1,000 kg/m^3, for short. Olive oil is less dense than water. Its density is

Layered lemon jelly

Ingredients
1 packet lemon jelly
250 ml boiling water
250 ml cold water
2 eggs

Equipment

a small bowl
a measuring jug
a tablespoon
an electric or hand whisk
a large bowl
a glass serving bowl or dishes

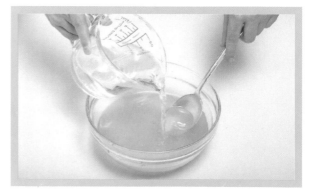

1 Break up the jelly into pieces and put them into the small bowl. Ask an adult to measure out 250 ml of boiling water and to add the water to the jelly pieces.

2 Stir until all the jelly has dissolved into the water. Add the cold water to the jelly and stir. Chill the bowl of jelly in the fridge for 1¼ hours.

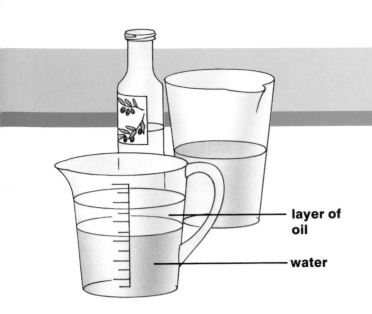

layer of oil

water

!

People in African markets use density to find out whether the eggs on sale are fresh. They put each egg into a bowl of water. A stale egg is less dense than water because it is filled with gas, and so it will float. But a fresh egg is more dense than water and will sink to the bottom of the bowl.

about 700 kg/m^3. Oil floats on water. Any substance that is less dense than water will float. Any substance that is more dense than water will sink.

3 Separate the eggs. Place the egg whites in the large bowl and whisk until stiff. Take the jelly out of the fridge and add it to the bowl of egg whites.

4 Mix together with a tablespoon and pour the mixture into the serving bowl or dishes. Return the jelly to the fridge for at least 2 hours until set.

What is surface tension?

Have you noticed how water drips from a tap? Each drop does not break up as it falls, but it collects together into a round shape. The surface of water, or any other liquid, acts as if it has a skin. This is called surface tension. It is caused by the molecules in the liquid's surface pulling towards each other.

The surface of the water in a glass tumbler is not flat. The water curves upwards where it meets the sides of the glass. The water molecules and the molecules in the glass pull towards each other. This attraction between the water and the glass makes the water pull itself upwards.

A cloth is made from long thin fibres that are packed close together. Cloths soak up spilled liquids because surface tension pulls the liquid up into the gaps between the cloth's fibres.

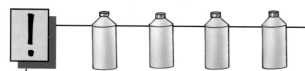

! Sprinkle a few drops of water onto a greased baking tray. Surface tension holds each drop in a tight round shape. Now lightly wet the end of a matchstick with washing-up liquid. Gently touch a drop of water with the stick. The drop immediately loses its round shape and slumps downwards, spreading over the tray.

Washing-up liquid is a detergent and causes the surface tension of water to become less. This helps water to mix with grease and to clean dirty dishes.

molecules at surface of drop pull towards each other

Mixing liquids

When you make a French dressing for a salad, you shake together a type of salad oil, such as sunflower oil, and vinegar and flavourings. This kind of mixture is called an emulsion. It contains droplets of oil which usually spread out through the watery vinegar.

Oil and water do not mix because the different molecules do not cling to each other. When you leave a jar of French dressing to stand, it slowly separates into two layers. The top layer is oil, which is less dense than watery vinegar.

Milk is an emulsion of fat droplets in water. The fat separates when the milk turns sour. Salad cream and mayonnaise are also emulsions.

You should not leave home-made mayonnaise for too long after making it. Mayonnaise contains an oily part and a watery part, which soon start to separate.

The mayonnaise that you buy in a shop keeps for much longer. It contains added ingredients called emulsifiers or stabilizers. They help the molecules in the oily part to cling to the molecules in the watery part. Emulsifiers stop the droplets of oil from joining together and separating from the watery part.

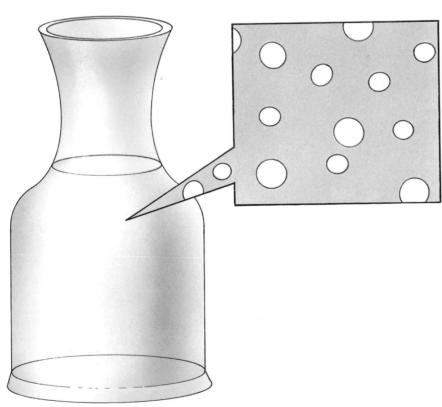

oil droplets spread out through vinegar in an emulsion

oil and vinegar droplets separate into two layers

Winter salad with dressing

Ingredients
225g white cabbage
225g red cabbage
3 sticks celery
1 punnet mustard and cress
½ teaspoon dry mustard powder
½ teaspoon salt
¼ teaspoon pepper
75 ml sunflower oil
25 ml wine or cider vinegar

Equipment

a chopping board
a knife
a large bowl
a pair of scissors
a sieve
a tablespoon
a teaspoon
a fork
a measuring jug

1 Ask an adult to help you slice the cabbage finely. Wash the sliced cabbage and put it into a large bowl.

2 Wash and chop the celery. Put the chopped celery into the bowl.

3 Use the scissors to cut off the mustard and cress. Put them in a sieve and rinse under cold water. Drain, and then add the mustard and cress to the bowl.

4 Put the dry mustard, salt and pepper into the jug. Add the oil up to the 75-ml mark.

5 Now add the vinegar up to the 100-ml mark. Whisk with the fork to blend together all the ingredients.

6 Pour the dressing over the salad. Mix well with the fork and spoon so that all the salad is coated with the dressing. Serve as soon as possible.

Acids and alkalis

Vinegar and lemon juice have a sharp taste. This is because they both contain substances called acids. Acids dissolve in water to make solutions that are acidic. Your stomach makes an acid that helps to break down and digest your food.

When you have too much acid in your stomach, this can cause indigestion. Some people suck indigestion tablets to relieve their indigestion. These tablets contain substances called alkalis. Alkalis dissolve in water to make solutions that are alkaline. The alkali from the tablets fights against the extra acid in the stomach and takes away its effect. The result is water and a substance like salt. Water is neither acidic nor alkaline. It is neutral.

You can use the coloured water from boiled red cabbage or beetroot as an indicator. Pour some coloured water into five glass jars. Stir one of the following into each jar: lemon juice, vinegar, bicarbonate of soda, baking powder and soap. Make a note of the colour of the liquid in each jar. Can you work out which substances are acids and which are alkalis?

The acids and alkalis you use in cooking are weak, but others are dangerously strong. Car battery acid can eat through metal. The alkali in oven cleaner can burn skin.

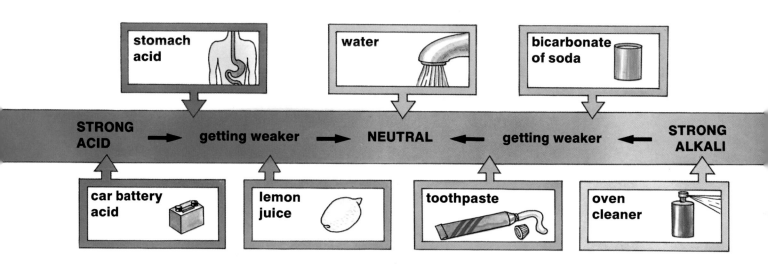

Scientists use special dyes, called indicators, to find out if a solution is acidic, alkaline or neutral. An indicator changes to a different colour, depending on the kind of solution it is placed in.

Fizzy lemonade

Ingredients

2 lemons
500 ml water
2 tablespoons sugar
½ teaspoon bicarbonate of soda

Equipment

a grater
a chopping board
a lemon squeezer
a measuring jug
a 750-ml jug (to serve)
a tablespoon
a teaspoon
a knife

1. Wash the lemons well. Grate the outer yellow rind on a fine grater. Put the rind into the glass jug.

2. Cut the lemons in half and squeeze out all the juice. Add this to the jug, making sure you leave the pips behind.

3. Measure the water and add it to the jug, together with the sugar. Stir until the sugar has dissolved. Taste the lemonade, and add more sugar if it is too sour.

4. Stir in the bicarbonate of soda and serve at once, while the lemonade is fizzing.

Further things to do

Take two identical plastic bottles and half fill each one with water. Dissolve a tablespoonful of salt in one bottle. Place both bottles in the freezer. Check as they begin to cool. The bottle of pure water will freeze first. The salty water freezes later, when the temperature has fallen. Solutions freeze at lower temperatures than pure water.

To show that vegetables contain water, seal some fresh lettuce leaves inside a polythene bag. Place the bag on a sunny window sill. After a few hours, the inside of the bag will be coated with drops of water.

Take a measuring jug and some glass jars of different sizes. Guess the volume of each jar in millilitres. Then fill one of the jars with water. Pour the water back into the measuring jug to see how accurately you had guessed. Repeat with the other jars.

Place a blunt darning needle on a small piece of kitchen paper towel. Lay them carefully on the surface of some water in a shallow baking dish. After a few minutes the paper will sink, leaving the needle floating on the surface skin of the water. Now touch the surface of the water with the end of a match that has been dipped in washing-up liquid. This reduces the surface tension and makes the needle sink to the bottom of the dish.

Half fill two glass tumblers with water. Put three tablespoonfuls of salt into one, and stir until the salt has dissolved. Place a fresh egg in the tumbler of pure water, and then into the one filled with the salt solution. The egg sinks in the fresh water and floats in the salt solution. Salty water is more dense than fresh water.

Glossary

acid
A substance that can make an alkali become neutral.

alkali
A substance that can make an acid become neutral.

atom
The smallest part of any substance. There are about 100 different sorts of atom.

boil
A change that happens when a very hot liquid bubbles and froths, and gives off a gas.

degree Celsius
A unit that is used to measure temperature. It is written as °C for short. The scales of most thermometers are marked in degrees Celsius.

density
A measurement that gives the mass of 1 cubic metre of a substance.

dissolve
When a substance mixes into a liquid and makes a clear solution.

emulsion
A mixture that is made up from droplets of one liquid spread out in another liquid.

energy
Energy makes things happen. Adding heat energy to a substance makes it become warmer.

evaporate
The way in which a liquid slowly changes into a gas or vapour.

filter
A piece of equipment that is used to separate the solid pieces mixed in with a liquid.

indicator
A sort of dye that changes its colour and shows if a liquid is an acid or an alkali.

insoluble
Describes a substance that does not dissolve in a liquid.

mass
A measurement that shows how much matter is in something. Mass is measured in kilograms.

matter
Everything in the world is made up from matter. Matter has mass and volume.

molecule
A tiny part that makes up most substances. Each molecule contains two or more atoms.

neutral
Describes a liquid solution that is neither an acid nor an alkali.

saturated
Describes a solution that has dissolved as much as possible of another substance.

scale
A row of marks with numbers that is used to measure something.

soluble
Describes a substance that can dissolve in a liquid.

solution
The liquid that results when a substance is dissolved in a liquid.

surface tension
An effect that makes a liquid behave as if it has a skin.

suspension
A mixture that contains a powdery solid shaken up with a liquid. The solid does not dissolve in the liquid.

volume
A measurement that shows how much space an object takes up. Volume is measured in litres.

Index